When We Can't See the Forest for the Bushes

Pat Oliphant

**Andrews McMeel
Publishing**

Kansas City

01 02 03 04 05 BAH 10 9 8 7 6 5 4 3 2 1

ISBN: 0-7407-1846-0

Library of Congress Control Number: 2001090066

──────── **ATTENTION: SCHOOLS AND BUSINESSES** ────────

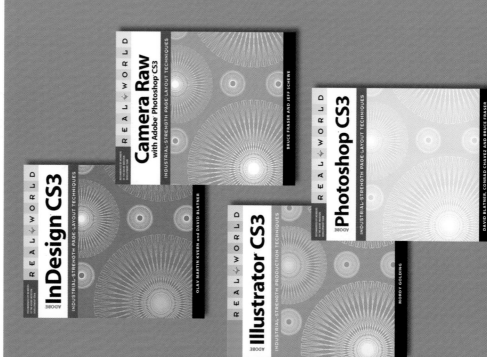

Recent Books by Pat Oliphant

October 17, 2000

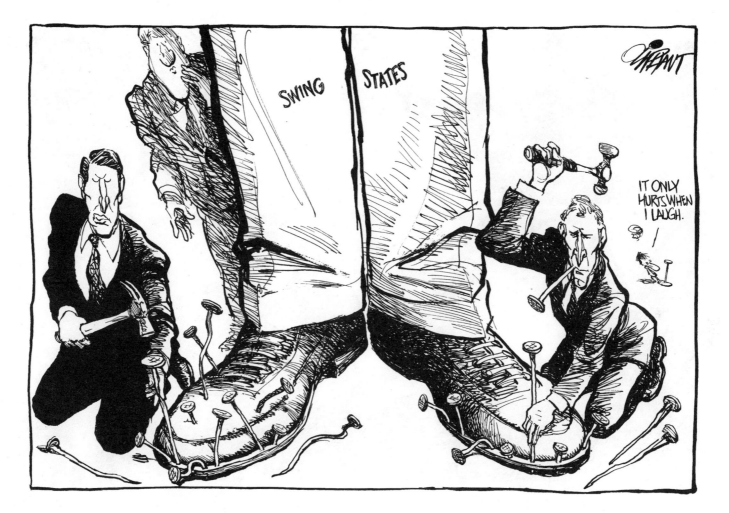

ALBERT and the dreaded NADERMAN.

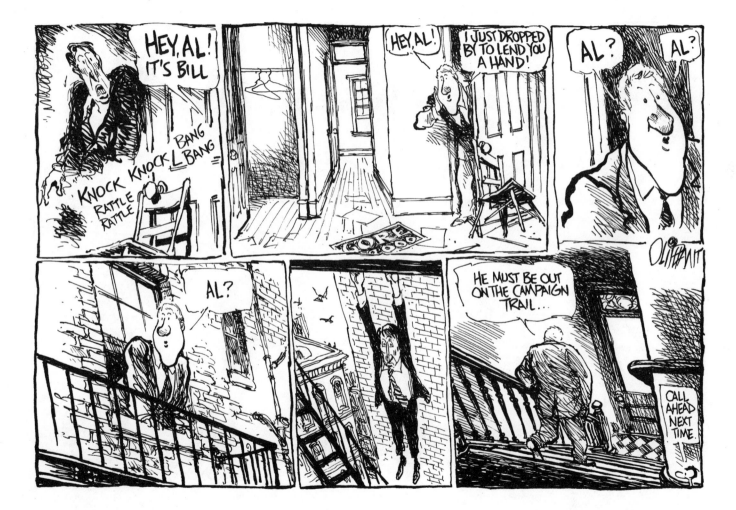

November 9, 2000

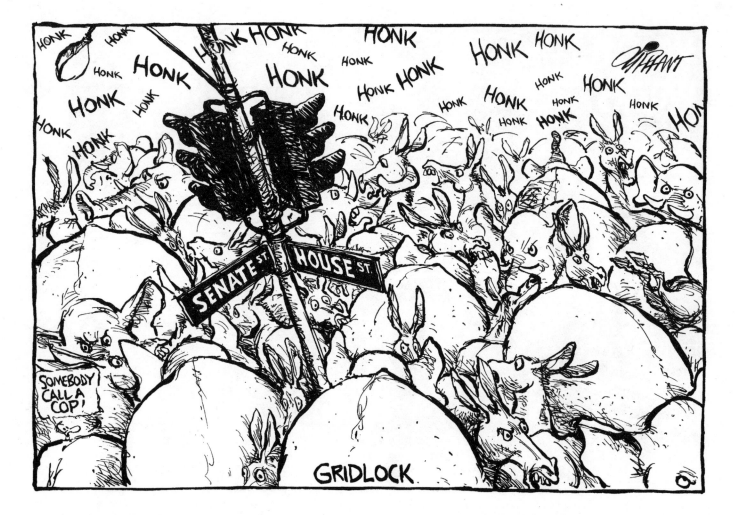

The train from Tallahassee, previously due to arrive at 9am, shall now arrive at 5pm.
The train from Tallahassee, previously due to arrive at 5pm, may now arrive at 10pm.
The train from Tallahassee, previously due to arrive at 10pm today, may now arrive at 12 noon tomorrow.
Or not, depending on what your interpretation of "shall" and "may" is.

ELECTORAL SYSTEM R.R.

ESRR

HELLUVA WAY TO RUN A RAILROAD

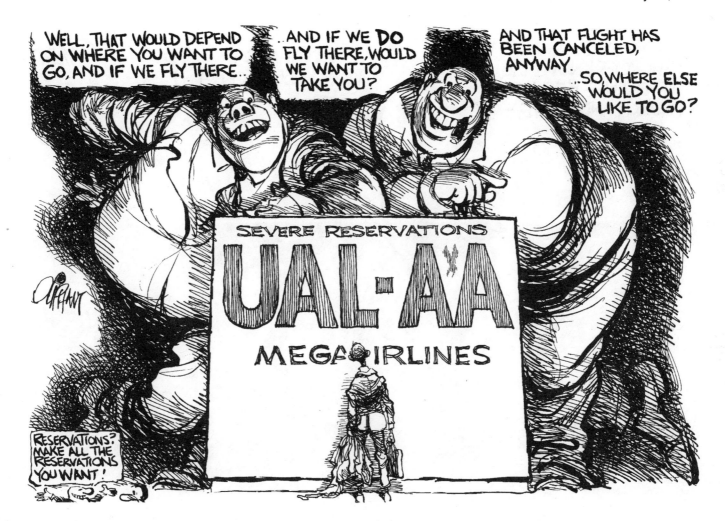

January 16, 2001

February 6, 2001

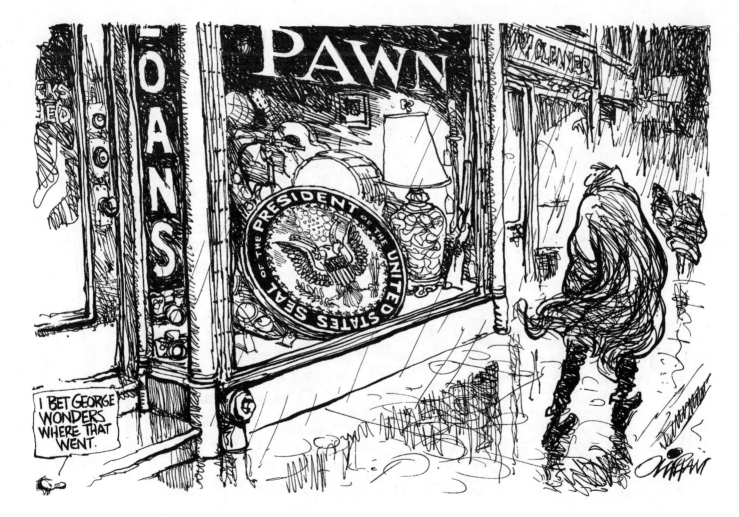

AND NOW...THE WORLD'S GREATEST TAP-DANCER PLAYS HARLEM!

THERE GOES THE NEIGHBORHOOD!

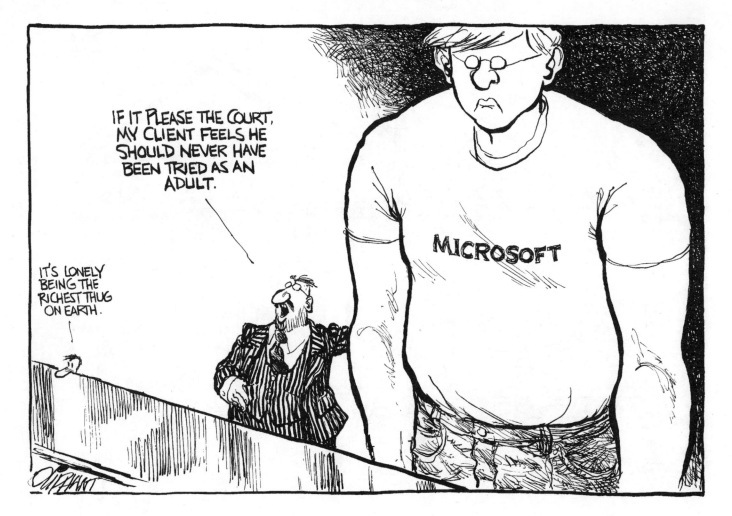

March 7, 2001

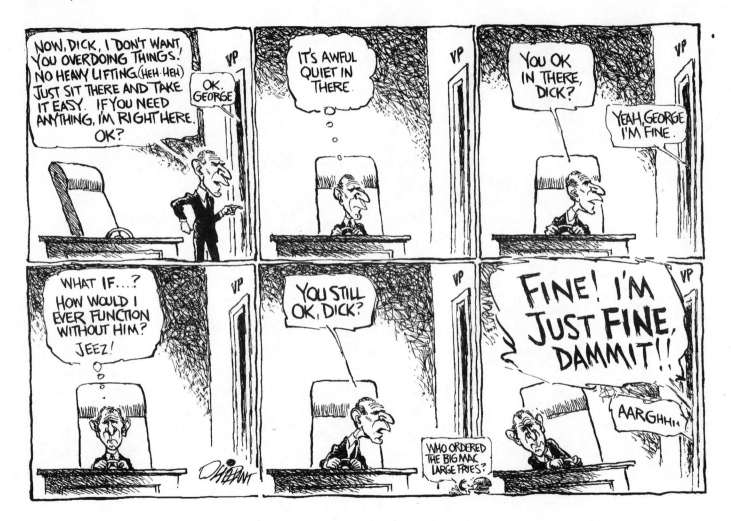

March 16, 2001

March 19, 2001

63

March 26, 2001

April 24, 2001

76

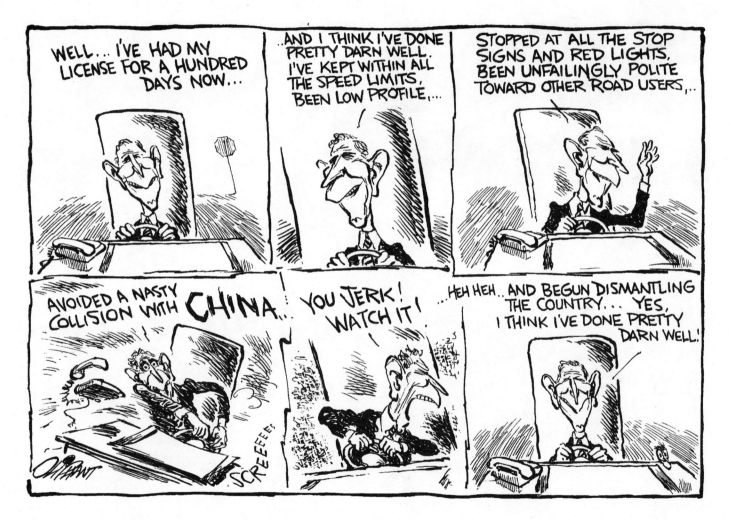

May 1, 2001

May 23, 2001

June 6, 2001

July 12, 2001

105

August 22, 2001

September 19, 2001

120

October 22, 2001